Evaporation, Transpiration and Precipitation

Water Cycle for Kids | Children's Water Books

I n this book, we're going to talk about the water cycle. So, let's get right to it!

WHAT IS THE WATER CYCLE?

The water cycle, also called the hydrologic cycle, is an amazing process. If you've ever looked up at the sky and seen clouds that were really dark, you could tell that they were filled with water. Soon, a thunderstorm might be happening and when it does, rainwater will pour from the sky. Did you ever wonder how that water got up there in the first place?

ater goes through a process where it collects in waterways on Earth or in the soil or ground. Then, it evaporates and goes up into the atmosphere again. There are many different stages in the process of the water cycle. There's really no beginning and no end to the cycle. Water is continually moving through the various stages at different places on the Earth's surface.

STAGE 1

Evaporation of water and
transpiration of plants

You may have noticed that when you were heating up water on the stove, it turns into steam and then evaporates into the air. The same process of evaporation happens every day on the surface of the oceans and other large bodies of water. As the rays of the sun shine down on these water surfaces, the water heats up and then begins to change to vapor and goes into the air.

The other way that water gets into the air is from plants. All green plants emit moisture by transpiration. The moisture they give off

also goes into the air as vapor. Currents of air gradually lift the water vapor up into the higher atmosphere.

Condensation

As the vapor goes higher into the atmosphere it begins to get cooler. The vapor starts to transform back into its liquid form of water. The wind and the masses of air stir this moisture and eventually this motion of the wind and air forms clouds. Over time, some clouds get heavy because they contain more moisture than other clouds. If enough moisture gathers, the cloud is ready to release its moisture either as rain or in another form.

Precipitation

The clouds release their moisture and depending on many different factors this precipitation falls down to Earth's surface in liquid form as rain or as other semi-solid or solid forms, such as ice pellets and snow.

STAGE 4

Runoff on the ground surface
as well as infiltration into the ground

As the water falls on the surface of the Earth, the force of gravity and sloping surfaces allows it to collect or runoff into puddles and other waterways such as streams.

Eventually, the water runs into the oceans and other large bodies of water that started the Stage 1 part of the process.

Depending on how water-saturated the soil already is, the water absorbs into the surface of the soil. This absorption into the soil is called infiltration. Sometimes the water goes down deeper and replenishes other water sources that are located quite a distance under the Earth's surface. This deeper penetration to underground water is called percolation. Sometimes ground water comes back up to the surface again and can either evaporate or runoff.

Let's look at these stages in more detail.

EVAPORATION

The sun is critical to the process of evaporation. Without the energy from the sun, there wouldn't be a water cycle. The sun's rays and warmth are necessary to heat water to the boiling point so that it can transform into vapor, which is a gas.

ater starts to boil when it is heated to the temperature of 212 degrees Fahrenheit, which is 100 degrees Celsius. Water is the

compound H2O in its liquid state and heating it to boiling transforms it into vapor by breaking the bonds between the water molecules.

The surface of the Earth is about 70% water. This vast surface area soaks up the heat from the sun. Scientists believe that most of the atmosphere's moisture, about 90%, comes from evaporated water from the five oceans as well as lakes and other waterways.

The amount of water that goes into the atmosphere from evaporation is more than the precipitation that falls from the clouds back

down to Earth. On the other hand, there is less moisture that evaporates from the land's surface than what falls in precipitation, so it balances out.

At times, solid particles of ice can transform into gas without changing into a liquid first. This happens a lot in dry climates, where desert winds striking snow absorbs its moisture, which turns the snow into vapor directly. This process is described as sublimation.

About 90% of the air's moisture comes from evaporation and the other 10% comes from transpiration of plants.

TRANSPIRATION

If you want to see how transpiration works, just use a plastic bag to cover up one of the leaves of a plant. After a while, you'll notice that the bag looks kind of steamy. This is due to the plant letting out moisture. Plants absorb water through their roots and let water vapor out from pours on the underside of their leaves.

CONDENSATION

You've probably witnessed condensation many times but may not have known what it was. If you boil some water on the stove and then put a dry lid on top of the boiling pot, something interesting happens. When you lift up the lid, you'll see droplets of water running down the lid and falling back into the water in your pot.

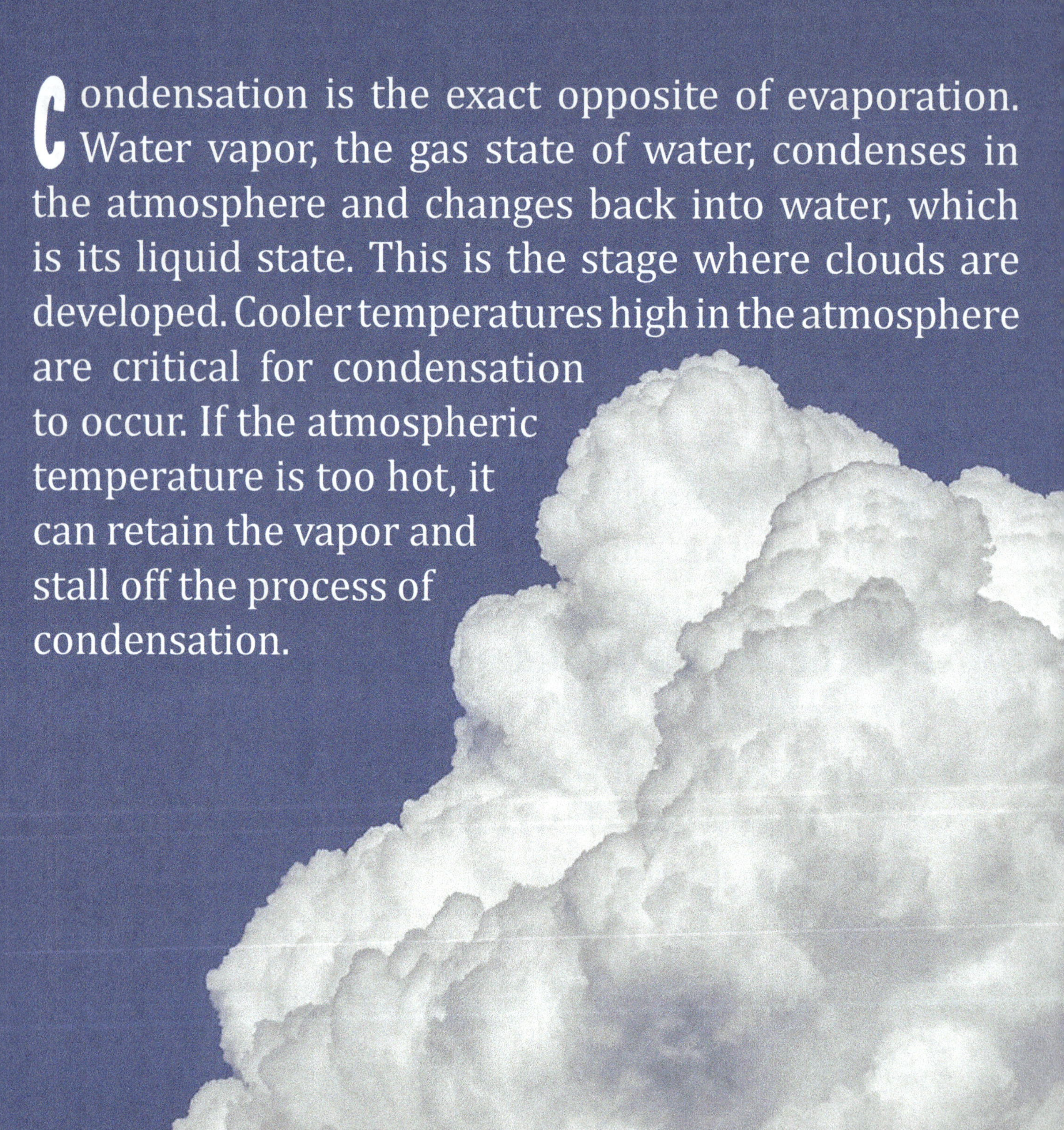

ondensation is the exact opposite of evaporation. Water vapor, the gas state of water, condenses in the atmosphere and changes back into water, which is its liquid state. This is the stage where clouds are developed. Cooler temperatures high in the atmosphere are critical for condensation to occur. If the atmospheric temperature is too hot, it can retain the vapor and stall off the process of condensation.

As the vapor rises, it mixes with dust particles as well as soot and crystals of salt. As temperatures drop, the vapor changes into small particles of water as well as ice crystals. As these particles of water continue to crash into the other types of particles, they begin to stick together to create clouds. Coalescence is the name of this process. The water droplets that clouds are composed of are as small as 10 microns and as large as 1 millimeter in size.

Eventually, the atmosphere gets so saturated with water that it must come down from the clouds in the form of precipitation.

PRECIPITATION

The most common form of precipitation is rain, but when the weather is very cold, precipitation can come down in the following forms:

- Freezing rain
- Snow
- Sleet
- Hail

Moisture in the atmosphere sometimes shows up as fog as well.

After the process of condensation occurs, the water droplets in clouds continue to get larger and larger as they crash into each other. Soon the pull of gravity on these weighty water droplets is stronger than the force of the wind and air holding them up. There's nowhere left to go but to come down on the surface of the Earth.

The amount of precipitation that falls varies greatly depending on where you are on Earth. Some regions get a lot of precipitation and others get very little.

he tiny particles that are composed of dust, salt crystals, and soot are very important to the way that water droplets form. They create a

central core where the water will gather. Because of this, rainwater is rarely pure but instead has minerals and other impurities in it.

RUNOFF

If precipitation doesn't get into the soil or doesn't evaporate, then it forms runoff. The water travels along the ground into places where it collects. Runoff sometimes causes soil erosion as the water carries away topsoil with it as well as chemical substances that may be there. Because of this, runoff sometimes causes pollution.

S cientists estimate that about 65% of the water that falls is absorbed by soil and the other 35% eventually ends up in a large waterway, such as an ocean or sea.

Those percentages aren't exact since some precipitation evaporates as well. The terrain of a region and its rock composition has a lot to do with how much runoff there is.

INFILTRATION

Most rainwater and snow ends up in the surface of the ground and soaks through soil and rocks as well as the cracks and porous spaces between them. If there are a huge number of plants or other vegetation, they soak up a lot of the water. Non-porous rocks and soil won't absorb as much of the water as those that are porous. Depending on how much water saturation the ground has, the water will at times continue to percolate downwards and increase the amount of underground water.

SUMMARY

The water cycle is an amazing process consisting of evaporation, transpiration, condensation, precipitation, and infiltration. The sun's warmth is essential to the water cycle. Liquid water changes to a gas, which is called water vapor, and then rises into the atmosphere. Eventually, the water comes back down to Earth in the form of either liquid rain or as partially solid forms of precipitation such as freezing rain, snow, sleet, or hail.

Awesome! Now that you've read about the water cycle you may want to read about water pollution in the Baby Professor book *Did Your Can of Soda Kill A Whale? Water Pollution for Kids | Children's Environment Books.*

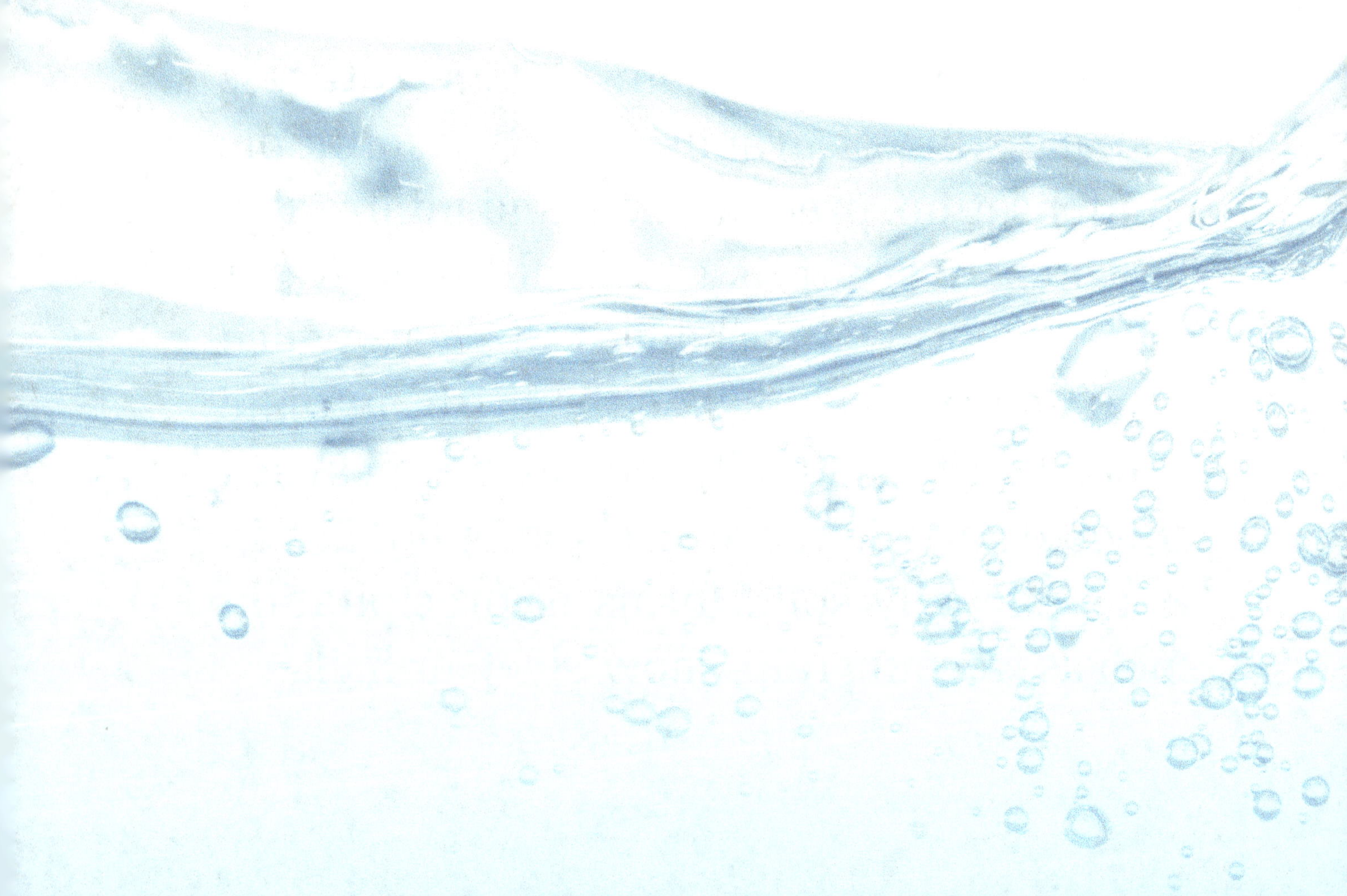

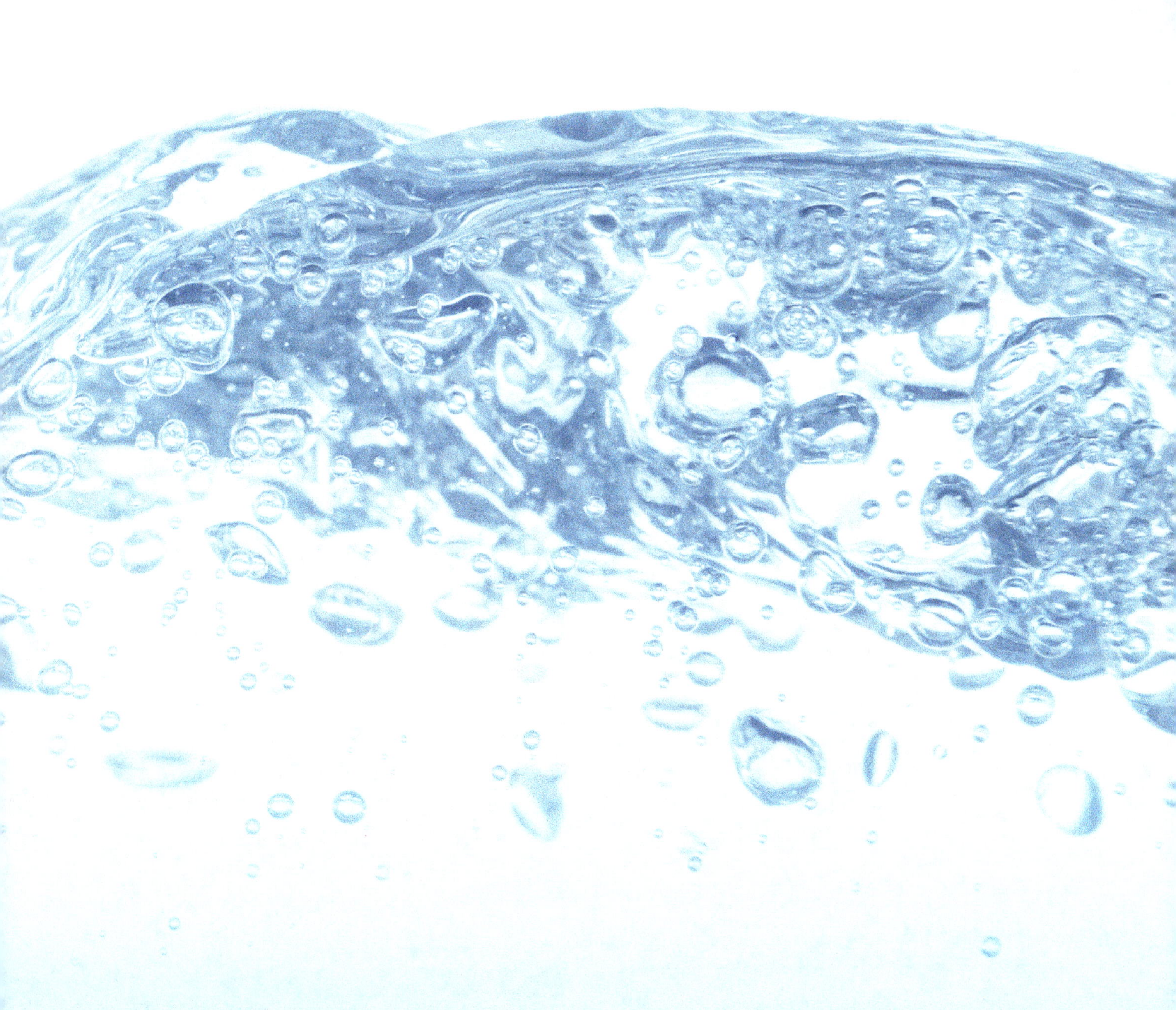

Visit

BABY PROFESSOR
EDUCATION KIDS

www.BabyProfessorBooks.com

to download Free Baby Professor eBooks
and view our catalog of new and exciting
Children's Books